FLYING FOXES
ARE NOT FOXES!

Jamie Honders

Gareth Stevens
PUBLISHING

Please visit our website, www.garethstevens.com. For a free color catalog of all our high-quality books, call toll free 1-800-542-2595 or fax 1-877-542-2596.

Library of Congress Cataloging-in-Publication Data

Honders, Jamie.
Flying foxes are not foxes! / by Jamie Honders.
    p. cm. — (Confusing creature names)
Includes index.
ISBN 978-1-4824-0784-6 (pbk.)
ISBN 978-1-4824-0939-0 (6-pack)
ISBN 978-1-4824-0783-9 (library binding)
1. Bats — Juvenile literature. 2. Flying foxes — Juvenile literature. I. Honders, Jamie. II. Title.
QL737.C575 H66 2015
599.4—d23

Published in 2015 by
Gareth Stevens Publishing
111 East 14th Street, Suite 349
New York, NY 10003

Copyright © 2015 Gareth Stevens Publishing

Designer: Michael J. Flynn
Editor: Greg Roza

Photo credits: Cover, p. 1 Nacivet/Photographer's Choice/Getty Images; p. 5 Erik Zandboer/Shutterstock.com; p. 7 Wassana Mathipikhai/Shutterstock.com; p. 9 (black flying fox) EcoPrint/Shutterstock.com; p. 9 (little red flying fox) Frans Lanting/Mint Images/Getty Images; pp. 11 (flying fox bat), 13 iStock/Thinkstock.com; p. 11 (red fox) Mark Bridger/Shutterstock.com; p. 15 Janelle Lugge/Shutterstock.com; p. 17 Four Oaks/Shutterstock.com; p. 19 Nathape/Shutterstock.com; p. 21 Markuso/Shutterstock.com.

Printed in the United States of America

CPSIA compliance information: Batch #CS15GS: For further information contact Gareth Stevens, New York, New York at 1-800-542-2595.

CONTENTS

A Fox That Flies? No Way!. 4

Furry Flyers. 6

Big Bats, Little Bats 8

Like a Fox! 10

Where They Live 12

Topsy-Turvy! 14

Fruit Feast 16

Dinner for One? 18

Megabats!. 20

Glossary. .22

For More Information 23

Index 24

Boldface words appear in the glossary.

A Fox That Flies? No Way!

Have you ever seen a fox that could fly? Of course not! Foxes don't have wings. But you may have seen a bat named a flying fox. They look a bit like foxes. That's how they got their name.

Furry Flyers

Like all bats, flying foxes are **mammals**. Their heads and bodies often look like other furry mammals—such as dogs or foxes. But they also look a little like birds! The skin between their fingers, arms, legs, and body forms wings.

7

Big Bats, Little Bats

Flying foxes are among the biggest bats in the world. The largest weigh close to 2.5 pounds (1.1 kg) and can have a **wingspan** of about 6 feet (1.8 m)! Others are smaller. The dwarf flying fox only weighs about 4.2 ounces (120 g).

little red flying fox

black flying fox

9

Like a Fox!

Some bats look really creepy, but flying foxes are cute! Most have large bodies that look more like a fox's than a bat's. Many have reddish-brown fur. Their pointed ears, small eyes, and **snout** make them look like foxes, too.

flying fox bat

red fox

Where They Live

Flying fox bats live in warm areas in the Eastern **Hemisphere**. They can be found in Madagascar, Southeast Asia, Australia, and on islands throughout this area. They don't live anywhere near the United States, which is in the Western Hemisphere.

Asia

Australia

Madagascar

13

Topsy-Turvy!

During the day, flying foxes roost in the tops of tall trees. A roost may have hundreds, thousands, or tens of thousands of flying foxes. The bats grab a branch with their feet. Then they hang upside down. That's how they sleep!

Fruit Feast

Many kinds of bats eat bugs. However, flying foxes only eat plants. Large flying foxes use their sharp teeth to break open fruit and even coconuts. Some use their long tongue to lap up **nectar**. They sometimes eat leaves and flowers, too.

Dinner for One?

At night, flying foxes go out in search of food. Once they find a **source** of food, they'll come back to it every night until the food is gone. Flying foxes don't always like to share. They often eat alone or in small groups.

Megabats!

Big flying foxes and other big bats are sometimes called megabats. The largest bat in the world is the large flying fox. It can be very noisy. Many bats use their hearing to fly at night. However, the large flying fox uses sight and smell to find its way.

Get to Know the Large Flying Fox

fur coloring
dark red, orange, black, white

wingspan
up to 6 feet (1.8 m)

weight
up to 2.5 pounds (1.1 kg)

life span
15 years (up to 30 years in zoos)

diet
Large flying foxes are frugivores. Those are animals that mainly eat fruit. They also eat flowers, nectar, and leaves.

Fun Fact!
Just like bees, large flying foxes help new plants grow by carrying pollen from plant to plant. Sometimes they help new plants grow on islands many miles away from where they stopped to eat.

GLOSSARY

hemisphere: one-half of Earth. North America is in the Western Hemisphere.

mammal: a warm-blooded animal that has a backbone and hair, breathes air, and feeds milk to its young

nectar: a sweet liquid made by flowering plants

snout: an animal's nose and mouth

source: where something can be found

wingspan: the length between the tips of a pair of wings that are stretched out

FOR MORE INFORMATION

BOOKS

Britton, Tamara L. *Flying Fox Bats.* Edina, MN: ABDO, 2011.

Markle, Sandra. *Bats: Biggest! Littlest!* Honesdale, PA: Boyds Mills Press, 2013.

WEBSITES

Bat Conservation International
batcon.org
This group is working to keep bats around the world safe from harm.

Little Red Flying Fox
animals.nationalgeographic.com/animals/mammals/little-red-flying-fox/
Read about the little red flying fox of Australia.

World's Weirdest: Flying Foxes
video.nationalgeographic.com/video/animals/mammals-animals/bats/weirdest-flying-fox/
Watch a short video about flying foxes in Australia.

INDEX

Australia 12
black flying fox 9
dwarf flying fox 8
ears 10
Eastern Hemisphere
    12
eyes 10
flowers 16, 21
fruit 16, 21
fur 10, 21
large flying fox 16,
    20, 21
leaves 16, 21
little red flying fox 9

Madagascar 12
mammals 6
megabats 20
nectar 16, 21
plants 16, 21
roost 14
snout 10
Southeast Asia 12
wings 4, 6, 8, 21